Life Skills for Kids in a Digital World

Navigating the Foundational Life Skills Needed for Digital Literacy, Online Safety, and Privacy

Amy Daniels

Table of Contents

Introduction

Would you believe me if I told you that you are growing up in a completely different world than your parents? If you were born after the early 2000s, you are part of the *digital generation*, and that's really cool. What does it mean? Well, it means that everything in your life from the day you were born, including your birth certificate, is completely digital. It's stored electronically in a computer run by the state in which you live.

Why is it so cool to be part of the digital generation? Well, when your parents were kids, there weren't cell phones. They didn't email or text friends, and they couldn't ask Alexa or Siri any questions. People had to go to the library, read newspapers, and watch the news to research a subject or know what was going on in the world. Back then, If you wanted to listen to music, you had to put a cassette tape into a player or put a record on a special device that could play it. There were only a few songs on them and we'd have to go to the music store to buy new records, cassettes, or CDs, ask your parents to explain. Can you even imagine living in a world without cell phones? Sounds prehistoric, right?

Having a small computer in the palm of your hand is a pretty new concept, especially if you think about the fact that humans have been on Earth for thousands of years, but you are the first generation to be completely digital.

You are paving the way for everyone after you to use digital technology to enhance their lives. As humans, we never go backward in our evolution, so technology is here forever and will only continue to get better and more powerful. The online world has many cool things to make your life easier and fun. But it also has dangerous places that can hurt you without you even knowing it. I want to help you learn to keep your secrets safe and not become a victim to people with bad intentions.

Wait, do I even know what I'm talking about? After all, I didn't grow up with technology like you. Well, I have a young teenager who is also navigating the same digital world as you. We think our teenager is lucky because his mom has spent her entire adult career in the cyber security industry, helping companies keep their data safe, and his dad is a policeman. So, we know a thing or two about physical security and digital security.

Okay, back to keeping your secrets safe and avoiding becoming a victim. Those are the two most important things I want you to remember every time you interact with the online world.

You probably know some of what I'm going to share with you already. But if you could learn something new that you didn't know before, it would be worth it, right? So, what's in store for you? Here are a few of the things we will talk about:

- **Keep your secrets safe:** Guard your personal information like it's part of a secret superhero identity. Your full name, address, and school are your secrets, so keep them safe from others. We'll also learn about common online scams.

- **Stranger danger:** Imagine the internet as a world filled with awesome friends but also some dark characters who may want to trick you. Never meet someone from the internet without telling your parents. People aren't always who they say they are, and this is dangerous because it means bad things could happen to you.

- **Outsmart the cyberbullies and trolls:** Cyberbullies are like the villains of the online world. If someone's mean to you, don't fight them alone. Tell trusted grown-ups, like your parents, about what's happening. They can help you report these people to the right places that will deal with them.

- **Pick safe websites and games:** Only hang out on websites, games, and apps your parents or possibly older siblings say are safe. They have more experience with these types of things, so you should listen to them.

- **Manners matter:** Imagine the internet as a big, digital party, play date, or other fun event. Be a good party guest—use your best manners and be friendly to everyone.

- **Social media knowledge:** Let's keep it all in perspective.

- **Balance the fun:** Remember you must balance screen time and regular playtime. Go outside, read books, and have real-world adventures with your fabulous friends. You'll just become tired and lazy if you sit in front of screens all day.

- **So you want to be a gamer or influencer:** What's possible for future jobs?

Why you might not like some parts of this book:

Have you ever read a book where the author admitted you might not like it? I must sound like I'm nuts. But hear me out…

We all have things we don't like but must do anyway. I always tell my son, let's get done with what we *have* to do so we can then do what we *want* to do. Even adults have things they do because they have to, even though they really don't want to. They are not fun; they don't make us laugh and take way more energy than we have to give sometimes. Tell me if you can relate: When I was a kid, I absolutely hated homework. Especially spelling because my mom made me write every word 25 times every night. She did this because I had terrible grades in spelling. After I started writing them over and over every night, I got 100% on my tests. Back then, I thought my mom was so unfair and it was like a cruel and unusual punishment.

Now that I'm an adult, I still have things I have to do that feel like a cruel and unusual punishment. For example, would you believe I really, really dislike emptying the dishwasher? Obviously, if I didn't, it would always be full and I couldn't put more dishes in. That's somewhat of a silly example, but I'm sharing this because even though this book may not make you laugh or be considered fun, it's still really important. If I can get you to look at your digital world just a little differently, it might keep some of you from making a mistake that could be a bad one. There will always be stuff you don't want to do or listen to because it's not fun. This book is like one of those things. It's not the most fun, and maybe you don't think it's very interesting, but it's still important.

Even adults don't listen to things they don't want to. That's partly why people still do things like smoke, spend long hours in the sun without sunscreen, or eat lots of junk food. It's a lot easier to do what we think is enjoyable rather than what might be best for us. You would probably much prefer to get on your game console and play your favorite game or scroll through your favorite social media site to see what funny things your friends are saying. But I encourage you to take time to read this book as well to arm yourself with the knowledge that might make a huge difference in your life...

Are you ready to embark on your digital adventure? We'll turn you into a true digital champion. Let's start our journey.

Chapter 1:

General Online Content

Would you leave your front door open with a sign outside that said, "Come in and take what you want?" Now that sounds crazy, doesn't it? Well, your online world should be kept just as safe as your physical world. Your passwords are just as important as the locks on your front door. Only you and your parents should ever know your passwords, and they should be difficult to guess.

But I'm getting ahead of myself. When you were little, your parents probably taught you about *stranger danger*, right? **Don't talk to anyone you don't know**, and definitely **don't go anywhere with them**. I know, I know, you're probably thinking I sound like I'm talking to a toddler. But the online world is much like that, except there are a lot more people who want you to become their victim. Not necessarily to physically harm you but to take advantage of you. There are *lots* of criminals online who want to get your info to sell it to make money. It's easy for them because they are hiding in their own homes and think no one can find them, which is sometimes true.

Imagine you are playing a video game, and you have to travel through different levels and different worlds to find a treasure. The treasure is whatever you want it to be, but you have to find it before you get to keep it. You have a shield of armor and weapons to help you stay safe on your journey. There are characters you meet along your journey who look like normal people wandering around doing their jobs and playing in the parks. Some of those characters look creepy, but some look kind and normal. Some try to take your armor, trick you into following them to a trap door, and make you feel bad about yourself by saying mean things to you. In order to win the game, you have to keep all of your armor and find a way to reach the treasure. It could be fun, but it could also be scary because what happens if you lose your armor or follow the wrong person and fall into a trap? The internet is much like this game, except when you make the wrong choice, you can't just turn off the game.

Don't Be Fooled Online

Remember when I told you your parents didn't have the internet when they were kids? Well, back then, when people wanted information, they had to go to libraries, read encyclopedias, watch the news, interview experts, and find research papers on their topic of interest. Those things had to be validated for correct data before they were printed. When the internet came along, it became so easy for anyone to post anything online. Since there isn't control over what is posted online, it's up to us to determine if what we are reading is real or not. This is really important because it goes back to the two things I told you to remember. Becoming a victim doesn't always mean by something bad or physically hurting us. Sometimes, it just means:

- **Don't** be fooled into believing something that isn't true.

- **Don't** be tricked into sharing your personal information.

- **Don't** be tricked into buying something you didn't intend to buy.

Those people trying to trick you are like the bad characters in our game.

Finding Facts and Ignoring Fiction

Ever heard about Bigfoot? For more than 50 years, people have believed there is an enormous 16-foot-tall gorilla-like man walking around, and people say they have seen his footprints ever since.

Conspiracy theories are like make-believe stories that some people come up with when they think something mysterious is happening.

Bigfoot is an example of a silly tale people still believe. And many more like it are floating around the internet.

Well, how do you know if what you are reading is true or not? There are many things you can do to become your own online detective. We will discuss a few to start with.

Check the Information Is Coming From a Good Source

We need to check if the information is from a good source, like a trustworthy website. We also need to use our critical thinking skills, which is like being a smart explorer, to decide if something is true or just pretend.

Review the Domain Extension

The first thing to review is the domain extension. That's the **.xxx** at the end of the website address:

- **.com** is the most common domain suffix and is usually associated with sites that want to sell you something.

- **.org**, **.gov**, or **.edu** are most likely reputable websites

- **.edu** means it's an educational institution or school

- **.org** means it's a non-profit organization

- **.gov** means it's a government organization

There are many different domains and new ones are being introduced all the time.

Check for Pop-Ups

The next thing to notice is whether there are pop-up windows that want you to click on them to see what they are about. Lots of websites get paid for the advertisements they include on their site. If a site has them, they likely are not a good source for true information.

Who Is the Author?

Look to see who the author of the site or text you are reading is. Is it an average person writing their opinions on a blog or a subject matter expert who has worked in or studied the topic

Is it the Real Website?

You also need to make sure you're on the correct website. Shady Characters often create scam websites with very similar names that could easily be found if you misspell the name of the site you're trying to reach. Scam websites always want to trick you into losing your money or secrets. They can also trick you because when you start to type a website address, your browser shows you sites like what you're typing, so you don't have to type the whole address. They often trick you into picking the first site that pops up because it looks like what you want. Always check the address of the site to be sure you are going to the correct site. Taking two extra seconds to be sure can save you from making a big mistake. Have you heard sayings from your parents that make you cringe? My mom used to always say, "It's better to be safe than sorry." Well, now that I'm a mom, I understand why she told me those corny things. And you will, too, when you have your own kids.

Chapter Worksheet

Read each situation carefully and choose the action that will keep you safe online. Write your answers in the open spaces that are provided.

How can you tell if a website or game is safe to use?

_____

_____

_____

_____

You find a website that promises a free game, but they ask for your full name, address, and phone number to download it. What should you do? Will you provide them with any information just to get the game?

_____

_____

While playing a game online, someone asks for your password to help you get more in-game currency. What should you do? Will you give them the password and keep on playing? Perhaps you should report them to the game's administrators?

_____

_____

How do you check if something is true before you share it online?

_____

_____

Chapter 2:

Keep Your Secrets Safe

In this chapter, we will look at how you can keep your secrets safe online. You don't know the people online like you know your family and friends. They might be friendly to you, but it's difficult to tell what they really want from you, and you need to do your best to stay safe.

Keep Your Name and Addresses Private

Your full name is your special name, known only to you and your loved ones. You should only share it with your family and friends and not with strangers who you don't know online.

Use a nickname or only your first name when you're online. Not everyone needs to know your full name.

You should protect your name like superheroes protect their true identities. Think of it as having a special power when people don't know your real name. It's a great idea to use a nickname or only your first name when chatting online to keep your true identity safe.

Your home is like your secret hideout where you're safe and sound. **Don't tell anyone your address when you're online,** as this can be super risky. Make sure you protect your home and don't tell people where you live on social media, even if you know them. Posting your address anywhere online is not safe because it's not really a private conversation if it's posted somewhere. People you don't know can find that data.

Your school is where you go to learn, grow, and have fun with friends. It might be fun to chat with others online about where they go to school, especially when you're playing online games where you can directly talk to people. However, this can be dangerous because **people aren't always who they say they are**. Someone might tell you that they're a 12-year-old boy who lives in the same country or city as you do, while in the meantime, they're actually an adult who wants to find out where you live.

You don't always know what people online want to do. Someone could tell you that they want to meet you in person so that you can be friends, but it's actually an adult who wants to harm you in some way. If someone keeps bothering you to give them these details, make sure that you tell a grownup about it.

Another interesting thing to realize is that even if you're talking to a friend from school online, there are other people who can listen and see what you're up to. **Never talk about where you live, go to school, or hang out even with your real friends**. People with bad intentions hang out in games with kids and listen to the conversations in hopes of learning something that will tell them about you.

It's also important to create a unique password for any site in which you create an account. **Passwords should not be easy to guess**, and only you and your parents should ever know them. Don't even share your passwords with your best friends. It's hard to imagine they might do something wrong with them, but there are lots of stories about things that have gone wrong, even among friends.

Phishing Scams

Pronounced "Fishing," these scams have been around for a long time but have evolved in different ways to try and trick people. A simple way to explain phishing is this: People will try to get our information by pretending to be someone or something else. They intend to get access to accounts usually for purposes of sealing money. Many of your accounts are tied to some sort of payment for buying legitimate things like your Microsoft subscription that your parents helped you set up to start playing some of your favorite games. Most accounts have some sort of "paid" subscription, even if it's only a few dollars a month.

People who target kids often do it through games or chat systems. They offer in-game money and pretend they are giving it away for free. Remember, nothing is free, so never fall for scams like this. Kids have fallen for such scams and had their entire accounts taken over, lost all their progress, and then their parents find fraudulent charges tied to the credit card on the account.

Let's talk about a few common scams to be aware of:

- **Online shopping scams:** These sometimes can be promising products for really low prices, like a new iPhone for $15.00. You have to put your payment info in but you never get the product. You just lost $15.00 and now your payment info is out there.

- **Phishing texts:** These are phony texts you receive that appear to be from a real site like Facebook or Microsoft. They claim your account was compromised and you need to click the link to reset your password. Once you do that, they will have your login information. Never click on links that come to you in texts until you do your research to determine if it's legitimate. It's almost always a scam.

- **Money transfer scams:** This is when someone sends you a text and claims they sent money to the wrong account in error and need you to send it back. This is always a scam and you should never believe someone sent you money by mistake.

- **Pop-up scams:** Lots of websites have ads and things that pop up when you're looking at something. Many of them are fake and include links that actually download spyware or viruses on your computer. Some can actually capture what's called keystrokes or essentially follow what you type. They then get your login info and passwords to your accounts.

- **Clickbait:** This is another strategy used to get people to click on content. It can look like an interesting headline or thumbnail embedded into something else, such as a YouTube video you might be watching or an advertisement on a Website. Many times, it's just used to get you to click on it and drive page views to another site. Most of the time, the content is not accurate, nor is it even what was promised by the headline itself.

Catfishing

Have you heard this term before? It's very similar to phishing, but it plays on the human aspect of relationships with people. It's a very dangerous behavior that targets both kids and adults for various reasons.

Basically, someone creates an online profile for themselves, but all the information is fake. It could be a gamer profile or a social media profile. They make friends with people and sometimes spend weeks or even months pretending to be someone they are not in order to get to know another and gain their trust. Usually, the scammer will reveal their true intentions by asking to meet in person or asking for money.

Unfortunately, people fall for these scams all the time. One example might be asking for money to help them out of a jam. Another example might be getting someone to meet them in person because they intend to have a romantic relationship with them. This scam often targets kids because sometimes adults are mentally ill and like to be in relationships with kids. Or sometimes they want to simply take kids. They often pretend to be a kid the same age, then ask their new friend to meet them somewhere in person. This is extremely dangerous, and **you should never meet someone in person that you meet online**. Even if you feel like you can trust them because you've been talking for months, and you think they are a good person.

This is a pretty morbid topic, isn't it? While the chances of this happening to you are relatively low, you still need to be aware it's out there so you can be sure to fall victim to such deception. Your safety is most important. If you feel someone may be trying something like this with you, please don't keep it secret. Tell an adult you trust so they can inform the authorities.

How Emma Stayed Safe Online

Emma was a smart girl who loved to discover new things on the internet. She was also good at keeping her secrets safe online.

One sunny afternoon, Emma decided to play her favorite online game called Roblox. She had met a friendly fellow gamer named "StarGazer" a few days ago, and they became gaming buddies. StarGazer was fun to play with, and they chatted about their quests and adventures.

One day, while playing, StarGazer wanted to know what her real name was.

Emma remembered what she had learned and knew her real name was something that she should keep and protect. She enjoyed playing with StarGazer, but she didn't really know him, so she wasn't entirely sure if she could trust him. She thought for a moment and told StarGazer that he could call her GlitterGirl.

StarGazer seemed to understand and continued to chat about the game. Emma enjoyed their adventures, but she was always careful. She never told StarGazer her full name, address, or school, just like her parents had told her.

As the days went by, Emma and StarGazer continued to play and they had great adventures today. However, StarGazer then asked her where she lived and where she went to school.

Emma knew that she had to be firm about this, and she told StarGazer she couldn't share that information, as it was important to keep their important stuff safe. StarGazer kept on insisting that they were friends and that it was fine to share her information with friends.

Emma knew that real friends understood her boundaries and respected her online safety rules. She didn't reply to his questions and logged off from the game.

Feeling a bit uneasy, Emma told her mother about the situation with StarGazer. Her mother told her to be careful and not to interact with him again. She reminded Emma that her safety should always come first and helped her block that user so they could no longer find her in the game.

As time passed, Emma made more online friends. Some became her trusted gaming buddies, and she was always able to keep her personal information private.

Emma was able to continue her digital adventures while staying safe at the same time.

Chapter Worksheet

Read each situation carefully and choose the action that will keep you safe online. Write your answers in the open spaces that are provided.

If someone asks you personal questions online, what should you do?

_____

_____

You find a website that promises a free game, but they ask for your full name, address, and phone number to download it. What should you do? Will you provide them with any information just to get the game?

_____

_____

Do you think you have ever been the target of a phishing scam? What happened?

_____

_____

Have you ever looked at clickbait ads and then shared them? Why might it be bad to do so?

_____

_____

Chapter 3:

Social Media: Is It For You?

Are you already using social media? If you're on Facebook, Instagram, Snapchat, X (formally Twitter), and many others, you are already well ingrained in the social media world. These are platforms that allow users to become part of a community where you can share photos, ideas, messages, and much more. It can be a lot of fun because it's almost like joining a big friend group with people from around the globe. While social media is fun, you need to be careful when and how you use it, just like the rest of the internet.

The Pros

Do you know what *pros* are? They are what's good about something, so in this section, we're going to look at what's good about social media. It can be great if you use it in the right ways.

So why is social media so great? Social media **helps you stay in touch with your friends and family when you're away from them.** Maybe you've moved to a new place, and you can't see your friends as often as you like anymore. Well, through social media, you can share photos of your new life with them, chat with them, and see them through video.

Social media **allows people to build social networks.** The older you get, the larger your network will grow. As you get into your teen years, these networks can provide valuable support for people who experience exclusion (being left out) or have disabilities or chronic illnesses. Sometimes, just knowing and seeing others with the same challenges helps you learn how to cope with them.

Social media can also be like a big library. **You can learn about animals, science, and all kinds of other interesting things**. There are also funny videos and lots of other exciting things that you can explore.

It could potentially help you with your schoolwork as well, as it contains a lot of educational content. Platforms like YouTube Kids have educational channels such as National Geographic Kids or History Channel. You can watch videos that teach you just about anything you may be interested in.

Social media also **allows you to express yourself in creative ways**. There are various apps that let you create art and other videos.

Playing around on different social media platforms can also help you **improve your digital skills**. The more you become familiar with social media, the more you will be able to improve your online skills. Not only will you learn to navigate different online platforms, but you will also get to understand basic internet etiquette and learn how to use various features.

Social media can also **teach you about different cultures**, what they do, and how they see the world. You can learn about other people's languages and how they live. Together with your parents, you can look at travel bloggers and cultural educators on TikTok and Instagram. This will help you learn about different countries and traditions.

The Cons

The cons are what's negative or bad about something. You have to realize that while social media can be very fun and creative, it's not good for everyone all the time.

So, what exactly are those things that aren't great about social media? Let's take a closer look at this situation.

Sometimes, there are things on social media that aren't meant for our eyes. There might be things meant for grownups, and you won't fully understand them. They could also teach you things that you aren't ready to know yet and that you might find scary or might let you think you know more than you actually do. It's important that you stick to things that are right for your age. Remember, you have years to explore the adult world, while you only have a short time to be a kid. Your childhood years are some of the most important years of your life, which also create the foundation for your adult years. Don't spoil them by trying to be too grown too early.

Maybe you've been at a gathering with your friends when a rude person you don't know turns up suddenly and tries to spoil your fun. On social media, these could be the people who send you friend requests, but you don't actually know them. That's why you should only connect with friends and family members who you actually know. **You can never know what the intentions are of strange people who send you friend requests**. Often, these people have bad intentions, such as trying to scam you by asking you for money for something that you never get, or they could ask you for some of your personal details and then steal your identity.

Let's face it: **Social media can waste a lot of your time, even some of the fun things**. You're not going to learn anything by looking at funny memes all day. Watching funny videos could take hours of your time, and then you forget to do other important things, such as finishing your homework and playing outside with your siblings or friends. Everyone needs to find a balance between the time spent on social media and the other important things that need to be done in life.

Social media might encourage us to compare our lives to those of our friends, and then we end up being unhappy, even though we have a lot of great things happening in our own lives. You see, everyone shares the great stuff on social media, like when they do well on a test or they score a goal, but they don't like sharing the tough times. So, it might look like everyone is doing so much better than you, but it's not really the case. You might think other people's lives are perfect, but that's not the case either. Everyone has difficult times and challenges in their lives. If you start feeling jealous or sad about what your friends are sharing on social media, it's time to take a break from social media.

A study was done on more than 6,500 kids between 12 and 15 years old in the United States. It found that those who spent more than three hours a day using social media were at **greater risk for mental health problems, anxiety, and depression**. You're probably rolling your eyes right now, thinking to yourself that won't happen to you. But you may already be on your way to beginning some of those issues and you don't even know it. How cool would it be if you could help yourself avoid such challenges by knowing what *could* happen? It's never too early to take care of yourself so you don't become depressed by the time you're in high school.

We all like to post pictures of us with our family and friends. **Keep in mind that almost all pictures posted on social media have been touched up**. People use filters and applications to make themselves look better than they really do. Even adults do this. It can make us all feel bad because we wish we looked like other people. This usually bothers girls more than boys, but everyone experiences this at some point.

Sometimes, people make mean comments about things you may have posted or said while on one of these platforms. If you see mean comments, don't get too upset; it isn't your fault. If someone actively bullies you and continues to send you mean messages, talk to your parents about it and block them. **You don't have to let people stay part of your friend group or connections on social media**. It's also a breeding ground for rumors. Many rumors start on social media and then spread like wildfire because kids jump on board even though the rumors are likely false.

Just like you might see creepy strangers at the park, you could also find them on social media. **If someone makes you uneasy, don't interact with them**. Also, check with grownups if you're unsure if you should be friends with someone. Don't forget you can "unfriend" people at any time.

Tips for Using Social Media

You may think you know how to use social media, but the fact is we can all be better at it. So, let's look at some tips that will make you an excellent social media user.

Staying Private

Imagine your online world as your room. You wouldn't want strangers peeking in, right? Set your privacy settings to make sure only friends and family can see your stuff. Things like your home name and real address should always stay private. You have more power if everyone doesn't know everything about you.

Choose the Right Platforms

There are lots of social media platforms out there. Not all of them are good for kids, and some of them have age limits; for example, you have to be older than 13 to use them. Pick ones that are for kids and have stuff that you will enjoy, like fun videos, cool games and other learning opportunities. Also, get permission from your parents before you create accounts. They may only want you to use certain platforms, or they possibly don't want you to be on social media at all. TikTok has taken the US by storm and is an incredibly popular app. But did you know that the FBI and US Department of Justice launched an investigation into the company over fears they have spied on US citizens? The company that created TikTok is based in China, and some people believe they may be able to access more data than the users of the app might want. That's why it's so important to know who created the apps you download to your devices.

This is a very controversial topic, and I'm not going to tell you to use or not use the app. But I do think it's important to always see where the apps you use are developed and talk to your parents about using them before you download them.

Be Careful About What You Share

You can share cool events or social functions you took part in, but be very careful about what you share. Share the cool moments that made you smile, but keep some things just for you and your friends. Never share your friends' embarrassing moments, as this might damage your relationship, and they might not want to be friends with you at all. If you're not sure if you should share something where your friends are involved, ask for their permission.

Another mistake people make is sharing things like when they are on vacation. Did you know that when people's homes are broken into, it sometimes happens when they go on vacation because someone posted on social media they are gone, so criminals know they won't be home? Wait until you get home to show those cool pictures.

Be Kind and Respectful

Always treat people on social media how you want to be treated. Be kind to them, and don't be scared to use those colorful emojis. Tell a grownup if you see people bullied online.

Time Limit

It's a good idea to limit the amount of time you spend on social media. Set limits so that you have time to do other things. It's also a good idea to take an extensive break from social media and just stay away from it all for a while. So get out there into nature and enjoy yourself. Play sports, go on hikes, read books, do crafts, or any other activity that you enjoy. Life is about the combination of all your experiences.

Important Things You Need to Remember From This Chapter

- Social media helps you stay in touch with friends and family, especially if you've moved to a new place.

- Sometimes, there are things not meant for kids, so it's important to stick to age-appropriate content.

- Connecting with strangers can be unsafe; only connect with friends and family you know.

- Social media can consume a lot of time, affecting homework and outdoor activities.

- Comparing your life to others can make you feel unhappy. It's important to realize that people mostly share the good things that happen to them online.

- Social media attracts cyberbullies; tell your parents if you're being bullied.

- Just like in real life, be careful of strangers online; don't interact if someone makes you uneasy.

- Be careful about what you share online. Share positive moments, but respect others' privacy; don't share embarrassing things.

- Treat others as you want to be treated, and be kind and respectful.

- Set limits on social media and take regular breaks.

- Never keep online secrets; inform your parents if someone asks you to keep secrets.

Chapter 4:

Texts, Pictures, and Content

We all enjoy taking photos of the fun we have in life, like going to parties and events. Our phones and other digital devices also make this super easy. There are important things we need to remember when it comes to taking photos.

- **Before you even take someone's photo, you need to respect their privacy.** Don't take photos of your friends if they don't want you to, especially when they're in their bathing suits or doing something else that's private.

- **If someone tells you that they're uncomfortable with a photo you've taken of them, it's better to delete it.** If you share this photo on social media when your friend didn't want you to do so, this could hurt their feelings, even if you meant it as a joke. This is cyberbullying, and you should never do this.

- **Some photos could get you into trouble with grownups and even the police!** Remember, once you put your photos on the internet and other people also start sharing them, you can't get them back, and many other people will see them.

In America, you're only considered to be an adult once you turn 18. That's why there are strict laws to protect children.

You can find yourself in huge trouble with the law if you have revealing photos of someone who is younger than 18, even if you are also under this age. The law considers this as child pornography and this can mean serious trouble. If you have pictures on your phone, it can be considered "possession of," and if you send those same pictures, it can be considered "distribution of" child porn. If that is a new word for you, please ask your parents to explain. The reason I included this part of the book is because kids sometimes make mistakes and have these types of pictures without realizing it could be bad news for them. I want to help you to avoid it altogether so it's not something you ever have to deal with.

Even if you think it's just a private thing with a friend or someone you like, it can turn into a big issue. If parents see the photos, they might report it to the police, and that can lead to big trouble.

This is because there are really bad people who trade revealing photos of kids online. It's nearly impossible to get them back, and they could end up in a dangerous place on the internet called the dark web.

The way you speak to people online is much the same way. Whether it's a text message, social media message, or a good old-fashioned email, what you say matters. However, with electronic communications, there is always a digital footprint, and even if you delete it, there will still be evidence of it. Yes, some apps delete messages after being read but don't forget that all devices have the ability to take screenshots or even photos of other devices. Some parents have agreements with their kids to review their devices at any time. Don't say or send something you wouldn't want your parent to see. **You also need to be careful with your text messages, as they can also get you into trouble.** Once you click on the send button, other people can see and share whatever you sent them. If it's not something you would say in front of your parents, don't send it in a text message or post it online, either.

Emojis, Abbreviations, GIFs, and Memes (Content)

When we communicate online, we still use words, but our communication has also become a lot more graphic, as we use emojis, abbreviations, GIFs, and Memes. This makes our messages more fun and can also save us time, especially when we're typing on digital handheld devices that have smaller keys than our computers.

I'm sure you're already using emojis, abbreviations, GIFs, and Memes, but you may not know what they are called.

Let's take a closer look at these interesting forms of online communication and how they can make your messages more exciting and fun.

Emojis

Emojis are like cute pictures (some of them are cool) that you can use when you send messages to your friends or family on your digital devices. They help you say what you want to say to someone without using words. You can also use them to show your feelings, and many of them are also little faces that portray different emotions. While they initially started with just a few icons, there are now many different types available, and you should be able to find ones that can express what you want to say.

For example, if you're sad or happy, you can send them one of the faces that look like that.

Emojis make your chatting more fun, and they add color to your messages. Below are examples of popular ones:

 Face with tears of joy

 Heart eyes

 Smiling face with smiling eyes

Abbreviations

When sending messages digitally, we often want them to be short so that we can send them as quickly as possible. Below are some examples that can help you put together your messages fast. You probably know many of them already:

- LOL (Laugh Out Loud): This one helps you tell others that something is very funny and makes you laugh a lot.

- BRB (Be Right Back): You're going away, but you'll be back soon.

- OMG (Oh My Gosh/Goodness): You would usually use this when you're surprised.

- IDK (I Don't Know): You would say this when you're not sure about something.

GIFs

Graphics Interchange Format (GIFs) are moving pictures that are almost like short mini-movies. They don't have any sound, but they can show funny or cool things happening in a few seconds.

It's like a way to share feelings or make people laugh by using moving pictures instead of words. You can send them to your friends to show how you're feeling or to tell a quick story.

Social media uses GIFs to send quick messages to people. For example, you can send a happy birthday GIF to your friend on his birthday.

Memes

Memes are funny ideas that people share on the internet. They can be pictures, videos, or even just words.

Imagine you and your friends have a secret joke that only you get. Memes are a way to have fun and connect with others on the internet by sharing funny and relatable stuff. They are especially popular on social media platforms like Facebook and sent as emails. Just remember this is the same as texting and photos. It's always best to assume adults might see them at some point, so do use them if you aren't ready for the consequences of them being seen by someone other than your intended person.

The content we share online is very subjective. That means it's based on personal feelings, tastes, and opinions. Just because you think something is funny doesn't mean someone else will feel the same way. Human interaction is a lifelong learning experience and even adults find they sometimes send the wrong message.

In order to become successful adults, communication skills are a must. All this digital technology has created so many new ways to communicate but in some ways, it's made it more difficult. You see, when you talk to people online, via text, email, and so on, you're essentially having a one-sided conversation. You don't get the benefits of instant feedback like you would in a live conversation. What you say, what you post, and the memes and jokes you use can really bother someone. Or you may be the one who was offended and bothered by something someone else said.

Why are we talking about this? **Even though it may be a lot of fun to pick on friends online or send them a meme you found that is funny, it could get you into trouble.** Don't forget if you send something that might be considered offensive, that person will likely show others. They might even post it somewhere else. It will be seen by parents and teachers who may bring action against you. Always think about what you post before you send it. Could it hurt someone? Could it get you in trouble? It's better to keep it to yourself if you're not sure.

Worksheet: Exploring Online Graphics

Draw your own emoji or GIF in the open space below to show how you feel today. Color it in and share it with your friends or family! If you're not sure about the emojis, you can look at the examples above. You can find examples of GIFs online.

_____

_____

Why is it important to be kind and polite when using emojis and GIFs online?

_____

_____

Create a short story using emojis. Draw a sequence of emojis to tell your story. Share it with someone and see if they can understand your story.

_____

_____

Important Things You Need To Remember From This Chapter

- Anything you say or post online can and will be seen by many people, so be cautious of what you say.

- Once a comment or picture is posted online, it's almost impossible to take it down.

- GIFs are moving pictures without sound, conveying emotions, or telling short stories.

- Memes are funny ideas shared on the internet, including pictures, videos, or text.

- Enhances online messages by making them more exciting and fun.

Chapter 5:

Outsmarting Cyberbullies

You've probably had to deal with bullies at school. Maybe they've said mean words to you and even pushed you around, tripped you, or put notes on your back. These people usually aren't happy, and they take out their unhappiness on everyone around them. Many bullies pick on people they think are weaker than they are.

While it may seem like the internet is a safer place than in real life, we also find these bullies online. They are called internet trolls or cyberbullies. Trolls might even pretend they care about you for the sake of your health, but they actually just want to insult you and get you to react in a negative way.

Maybe you already know something about cyberbullies and internet trolls, but let's take a more in-depth look at them.

Cyberbullies and Internet Trolls

What Are They?

A cyberbully will use unkind words and actions to hurt you. Like in real life, they will say things to scare you or to make you feel worried or sad. While words hurt, they can't physically injure you, but they could still cause you to feel bad about yourself and cause you to lose self-confidence.

An internet troll is a digital troublemaker. They're like those kids at school who like to annoy the other kids and even the teacher. They post mean comments online and they enjoy starting fights. They can also say silly and hurtful things to get attention. Sometimes, they could even pretend they're saying something because they actually care about you. These are called concern trolls. These are the people who would make fun of your body, for example, because they think you're fat or large, and then tell you they're doing it because they care about you and they want you to lose weight so that you can be healthier. However, their true intent is mostly that they want attention for themselves.

What Is Self-Confidence?

If you have self-confidence, you believe in yourself, and you're able to see yourself as the awesome person that you are. If you have self-confidence, you enjoy trying new things, you're capable of learning from your mistakes, and you always bounce back with a positive attitude. You think you're great the way you are, but you also realize that you have to keep learning and growing in your life to make sure you're even more successful.

How to Deal With Cyberbullies and Trolls

Cyberbullies make negative posts in hopes of getting a reaction from the person they are targeting. Fortunately, on the internet, we can ignore or block them. Use your reporting and blocking tools to keep your online space free of these people; otherwise, many of them may continue trying to annoy you. Don't pay too much attention to their comments by continuing to post replies to their nasty comments. You don't want to become involved in a long fight in the comments with nasty people. It will only make you mad and put you in a bad light while they get the negative attention they've been looking for. It's best not to respond and simply block them so you don't see any more of their posts. Even if it's someone you thought was a friend, you may still want to block them because real friends don't make fun of their friends.

Another good idea is to keep records of the bullying messages you receive from these people. If a cyberbully says something mean, save their messages or take screenshots. That way, if they delete the text or post, you still have proof.

How Should You Treat People Online?

You should treat people with the same friendliness and kindness online as you treat the people you meet face to face every day. Be friendly and have a kind word for everyone you meet.

The following simple rules will also make the online experiences nicer for you and your friends:

- Be nice when you're playing online games, take turns, and don't be greedy.

- Listen to what others are trying to communicate to you. Wait for your turn to talk.

- Don't say hurtful things to others. Say nothing at all if you don't have anything good to say.

- Be careful what information you share, but also don't ask others for information that they might not want to share with you.

Libby Deals With a Cyberbully

Ten-year-old Libby was bright and cheerful and loved spending time online, playing games, and chatting with her friends. She made many friends online, as she was kind and helpful to everyone.

One afternoon, Libby decided to log onto her favorite game, which allowed her to explore magical worlds and complete quests. She could even team up with the friends she made online.

When she was about to join a game, she received a friend request from a player she didn't know, someone called "ShadowFax." She was curious, so she accepted the request. His messages were friendly at first, but as time passed, he started to send her unkind messages.

Libby's parents had taught her about digital safety and how she should deal with unpleasant situations when they happened online. She realized her friend was starting to behave like a bully.

She didn't respond to his mean comments at first, as her parents had told her not to interact with the trolls. She knew that ignoring the bully's messages would show him that she wasn't willing to be involved with his negativity.

She also told her parents, who reassured her that she did the right thing by ignoring him. They told her they would help her to handle the situation.

Libby documented all the mean messages she had received from the cyberbully. She took screenshots of their chats, as she knew she would have to provide evidence if she wanted to report him to the game administrators.

She also blocked him from sending her messages. It made her feel a bit better, knowing that she had control over who could contact her online.

Libby's parents also helped her to report the bully to the game administrators. She provided them with evidence of the situation and described how she felt threatened by his messages.

The game's administrators took her support seriously and they investigated the issue. Based on her evidence, the bully was banned from the game for violating the rules.

Libby continued to play the game and to have fun with her friends. She didn't meet any more cyberbullies, but she felt confident in knowing that she could outsmart them.

Important Things You Need To Remember From This Chapter

- Report cyberbullies and trolls to grown-ups and use blocking tools.

- Keep records of bullying messages, including screenshots.

- Concern trolls pretend to care about others, but they actually just want attention for themselves.

- Don't fight with bullies and trolls in the comments online.

- Be nice when playing games, take turns, and don't be greedy.

- Don't say hurtful things, and stay quiet if you don't have anything nice to say.

Chapter 6:

Artificial Intelligence

Artificial Intelligence (AI) is one of the newest parts of the digital world that is becoming very popular. If you have ever asked Siri or Alexa a question, you are already using AI. They both use natural language processing and machine learning to answer your questions like a human. Those are two parts of AI that make it work. It's like the brain of the computer figuring things out for you on its own.

This is a technical topic that can be super complicated. I don't want to bore you, but I want to try to help you understand a little about it.

It's like having a toy robot that doesn't have its own thoughts and feelings, but it learns from a lot of information that it has access to. Artificial intelligence learns fast, and it's always trying to learn new things. Like how you learn from your books and teachers, AI learns from information it accesses and prompts from users of the tool.

AI might seem realistic, but you must remember that it's not a real brain but simply a program that can learn and talk to you. There are some scary movies out there about AI coming to life, killing people, and taking over the world, but they are just science fiction movies. AI still requires human input.

If the information AI has learned is old, it might give you outdated information, and there are many cases in which the response is completely wrong. Do not consider anything you get from AI to always be accurate.

So, how do people use AI? Let's take a look at the many different ways in which you can use this technology.

How Do We Use AI?

Interacting with AI assistants can almost feel like talking to your friends. Siri and Alexa can tell jokes, answer your questions, and play your favorite songs if this is what you want them to do. It's really a strange feeling at first when you realize you're actually speaking to a computer and not a person, as some of the responses may seem realistic and life-like.

These AI assistants are funny and friendly. They'll even play you your favorite music when you tell them what you like.

These talking friends are like smart explorers. If you have a question about dinosaurs, the sea, different planets, or anything else, just ask them. They love sharing interesting facts and learning new things with you. It's like having a buddy who's always ready for new adventures and enjoys learning with you.

No matter what you're up to, your talking friend will make your day brighter and even more exciting. Whether it's telling you a funny story, playing your favorite song, or helping you with your homework, they're like your best friend who is always there to cheer you up. They use something called *natural language processing* to understand what you are asking, then respond with responses to your specific questions.

ChatGPT is one of the more common AI sites/tools. It was introduced in 2022 and had 100's of millions of users in just two months (Dickson 2023). It's an AI tool that lets you have natural conversations with a chatbot. You can ask just about anything and get very interesting responses. It can help you create emails, presentations, essays, code, translate different languages, and much more. Many people use the free version for all sorts of tasks. It's very important to remember that it can and does give wrong information sometimes and only knows the info already in it from its developers. It doesn't search the entire internet to find its responses. At the time of this writing, it was trained on data gathered in 2021 (Dickson, 2023), so the responses you get can be outdated and also won't have data on many current events. It's also very wrong to ask it to do your homework. While sometimes it can help you use your information to better organize or voice your thoughts, it would be cheating if you used it to do all your homework. And as I just mentioned, it can and does sometimes give wrong answers, so don't assume it will always be correct. It's really important to keep your secrets safe while using ChatGPT, so please never use anything personal like your name, address, birthday, etc.

Because AI technology is so new, and we haven't yet scratched the surface of how it might be ingrained in our lives, expect there to be controversy and new laws ahead that may limit and or regulate what we can and can't do with it.

Fun and Entertaining

AI has all kinds of fun and entertaining activities for kids.

Game Wizards

AI is a game wizard who watches how we play and makes the games more exciting. You'll have your own secret helper who knows all the game tricks.

Funny Filters

Have you ever used funny filters on Snapchat or Instagram? AI creates these scenes and adds things like cat ears or funny noses to our pictures.

Learning Languages

AI can also help you learn. It's actually a really cool teacher, especially for learning new languages. It can make your learning experience fun by giving you personalized lessons and games.

Helping Creativity

AI can also help you to be more creative. It can help us edit photos, suggest ideas, and even make your videos look better.

AI Platforms for Kids

Learning only from books in the classroom is a thing of the past, and the internet has opened many creative opportunities for learning. AI platforms can help you learn in interactive and exciting ways.

Scratch

Scratch is a visual programming language and online community where you can create and share your interactive stories, games, and animations.

If you're older than 8, this might be the platform for you.

Website: scratch.mit.edu/

Kodable

Kodable is a programming app that will help you learn coding concepts through fun games and activities.

This website is for kids from the ages of 5–8.

Website: www.kodable.com/

Microsoft MakeCode

Microsoft offers a free learn-to-code platform where you can learn how to build games, code devices, and even modify Minecraft.

Website: www.microsoft.com/en-us/makecode

Google CS First

Google CS First provides free, easy-to-use computer science enrichment materials for kids. They make learning easier for you by providing video-based lessons and coding projects.

This website is for you if you're from 9–14 years old.

Website: csfirst.withgoogle.com/s/en/home

Code.org

Code.org is a training platform that offers free coding lessons and activities for kids of all ages. It features themes from your favorite games like Minecraft and Star Wars to make your learning more engaging.

Various courses are available for different age groups.

Website: Code.org

AI Fun Worksheet

Answer the questions below about how AI can make your learning experience more exciting.

If you could teach your robot friend to do anything, what would it be?

_____

Do you want your robot friend to help you with any tasks? What tasks do you want them to help you with?

_____

If you could ask your talking friend to play any song, what would it be?

_____

If your robot friend could take you on an adventure, where would you go?

_____

What magical creature would you want to meet on your adventure?

_____

What's something new you would like to learn with the help of your robot friend?

_____

If you could teach your robot friend a fun fact, what would it be?

_____

Important Things You Need To Remember From This Chapter

- AI helps computers perform tasks, learn, and interact in a human-like way.

- AI doesn't have thoughts or feelings but learns from vast amounts of information.

- AI assists in learning new languages, creativity, and editing photos or videos.

- AI can and sometimes does respond with inaccurate data and should not be considered always true.

Chapter 7:

IRL—Time Away From

Electronics

We've looked at all the fun things that you can do online. You can play, create, and learn. Online gaming is attractive for many kids, and it's easy to lose hours playing exciting online games and scrolling through your social media accounts.

We know spending time online can often be more exciting than doing things IRL "In real life;" however, it's not healthy to spend all your time there, and you need to take breaks from time to time.

Before we look at why you need to spend time offline, let's look at what benefits playing games online can have for you.

Benefits of Playing Games Online

Playing games can make you smarter. Well, kind of. Some games usually need **problem-solving**, **critical thinking**, and **strategic planning skills**. So, playing online games can help you when it comes to having to make decisions in the future.

Online gaming can also be helpful for your **coordination and reflexes**. Many games involve fast-paced action, and you have to be able to think quickly and move with precision. It can also be a form of exercise if you're the type who likes to jump around while you're playing.

It's also a way to work on your **teamwork and social skills**. Multiplayer online games involve collaboration and teamwork. Kids learn to work together, communicate effectively, and understand the importance of collective effort.

This type of gaming is also a **creativity and imagination** booster. Games such as Minecraft encourage creativity by allowing you to build, design, and create worlds. If you're the creative type, once you get started with a game like this, you'll be hooked!

Goal setting is also important when it comes to these games. Games often have objectives and levels that players need to complete. This can help you learn about setting goals, and you can also feel the satisfaction of achieving them.

Gaming can also help you with your digital literacy and help you gain a **better understanding of technology**. You learn about using devices and understanding digital environments.

We've discussed this in the previous chapter, but educational games can also **make learning fun**. These games cover various subjects such as math, science, and languages.

It could also be your **way of relaxing**. It is stress-relieving if you're the type of person who doesn't get too upset about losing a game or two. It's simply a way to unwind by going to another world and taking a break from the daily pressures of your life.

Playing games can actually help you **become more resilient**. They're usually full of challenges and obstacles that you need to overcome, and this can help prepare you to face problems in real life.

Strange as it may sound, it could also help you **bond with your parents** if you're willing to play together. You can play some family-friendly games with all the members of your family. Maybe you even make game night a regular thing. I would also encourage you to try board games for game night. It's a lot of fun when you're looking at each other instead of a screen.

Why Do You Need Breaks?

This part is always a challenge for kids. After all, you've never known a world that isn't fully digital. However, many doctors and scientists have been studying the effects of technology on our health. This can often be very technical and probably quite boring, but it's important to understand. I'm going to share some of the findings but won't dig deep into the technical terms so I don't bore you right to sleep.

Struggle With Focus and Attention

Excessive internet use is associated with lower cognitive functioning and reduced volume of several areas of the brain (Ricci, 2023). In "kid's terms," it means you can actually be making yourself dumber. Some studies found people to be less verbally intelligent and have less volume in brain function in the parts of the brain that relate to language processing and attention (Mayo Clinic, 2022). That means it's a lot harder for kids to focus and pay attention. You probably know someone at school who struggles with this.

Poor Diet

Some studies reported that lots of advertisements for unhealthy and high-calorie foods, which you see online all the time, encourage kids to have a very poor diet, which we know can lead to being overweight and having health issues.

Affects Brain Development

Some studies show video games were associated with poor development of different sections within the brain. Without getting too deep into the weeds, if your brain doesn't develop naturally as it should when you are a kid, it likely won't ever. That sounds crazy, doesn't it? But it really is true, which is partly why there is a large increase in learning challenges with kids. I have to say, school is hard enough as it is; why would you want to make it even harder by messing with the development of the most important part of your entire body, which is your brain?

Some games are inappropriate for kids. Violent games affect your brain in negative ways. I know you probably think that sounds silly, but sometimes you just have to realize scientists and doctors who study these topics know more than you do. Do you ever think about what you knew when you were little and how much more you know now? The same is true for adults. We really do know a lot more than kids and you must trust the science that does lots of studies to understand how all this technology that your generation uses every day affects you.

Addiction

If you're always online playing games, you might be an addict. Addiction happens when you leave other things that you should be doing, such as your homework and sleeping, to play games. Your parents might try stopping you from doing things, but some kids will still try to find their way around this.

Schoolwork is Affected

If you spend all your time gaming, it could also lead to poor grades in school. Let's face it: If you're a hardcore gamer, it's going to suck your time. While gaming is fun, there are more important things that you should be doing.

Health Problems

Gamer kids could start to get health issues they would otherwise only have faced when they're older. This could be anything from eye strain to poor sleep. If it causes you to sit all day, you could also gain weight because you're not getting any exercise. Obesity is becoming a problem because it brings with it a lot of health challenges that never used to bother kids.

Breaks Down Relationships

While gaming could bring family members together, it could also force them apart. Relationships can be strained, and conflicts arise when children don't do their chores or they neglect their responsibilities because they would rather be gaming.

Gaming can teach you things, but it, unfortunately, could also cause you to lose very important real-world skills. That's why you need a balance between online activities and your physical, social, and creative offline social activities.

In-Person Communication Skills

Sometimes, you need to take a break from your electronics to step into the sunshine outside. Screen time may feel great, but too much of it is just as bad for you as eating too much candy.

When you sit in front of your screen too much, you become sleepy and sluggish. Going outside and playing will help you stay active and healthy. Your brain needs a break, too, as too much time in front of your favorite screens will just make you dull.

Your eyes will also thank you if you spend enough time taking breaks. Staring at screens for too long can make your eyes very tired and weak. Taking breaks and spending time offline can help your eyes relax. Studies have identified long-term impacts on your vision from too much screen time. When we look at something close and then something far away, our eyes know how to adjust very quickly, so we can see both because they have flexibility. As people age, this flexibility naturally weakens and they struggle to see far and very near. But kids who focus on screens for long periods of time actually cause this weakening at much earlier ages. So if you don't want to wear glasses to see far and a different type of glasses to see close up, please give your eyes a break throughout the day.

What Can You Do Instead?

Chatting with your friends face-to-face is important because it helps you learn how to talk and understand feelings without using screens. When you talk to them in person, you learn to recognize their feelings by looking at their facial expressions and what's known as "body language."

Reading facial expressions and body language is a skill everyone needs. When you're interviewing for college, a school internship, or a job, you need to be able to have a professional conversation with a stranger, or you will likely not be chosen. Kids who get practice talking to adults and others in person will always have an advantage over those who try to avoid it because they don't really know how.

One important reason why you should take breaks from technology regularly is to **spend time in nature**. Spending time outside in places like parks and gardens is super fun. It makes you appreciate the trees, flowers, and all the amazing things outside. Did you know that your body needs Vitamin D to be healthy? You get Vitamin D from the sun. Sunscreen is needed to avoid the bad rays that burn your skin, but sunshine is very important for our mental and physical well-being. Let's make a deal: You get to use your devices to do a search online about why kids need lots of time outdoors, and then put your device down and go outside.

Cutting your technology time will also help you **discover other hobbies** that don't have to involve technology. These could be creative hobbies like playing a musical instrument or drawing. There are countless activities to try that help build your imagination and are just fun to do. Ever tried creating something with papier-mache? Have you ever made your own Play-Doh? What about learning how to make balloon animals or creating a magic show? Ever tried to write your own book or create a story? Try it, then learn how to publish it yourself. Yes, some of these require supplies your parents might need to buy, but I bet if you tell them you'd like to find ways to be creative without technology, they would be excited to help.

And let's not forget about **sports**. There are both health and emotional benefits to playing sports. Oh great, here we go again with all these studies… I'm going to spare you a ton of details from all the studies but take my word for it. You will learn a lot more from playing sports, which you will take with you for the rest of your life. The physical benefits are usually fairly obvious, right? Sports make you more physically active, and we all know why exercise is important. But did you know there are also emotional and social benefits to sports (Mayo Clinic, 2021)? You learn about teamwork, as well as how to both win and lose together in the right way. Sports also help you to make lifelong friends, and in some cases, they may be different from those you see every day in class.

While technology is super cool and will continue to change in many exciting ways during your lifetime, it's important that you find balance and do other things as well.

Chapter Worksheet

Write down ways in which online gaming has made you more creative.

_____

_____

_____

What health issues can you develop if you play online games for too long?

_____

_____

Brainstorm some ideas to try that don't require anything digital. Jot down your ideas then actually try them.

_____

_____

Important Things You Need to Remember From This Chapter

- Too much gaming can cause health issues such as eye strain, disrupted sleep, and too little exercise.

- Balanced screen time is important for your mental and physical health.

- Outdoor activities will help you stay active, healthy, and connected to nature.

Chapter 8:

Pro Gamers, Influencers, and Jobs

If you had told me 15 years ago that people could make millions of dollars by making videos of themselves playing video games or trying on new clothes, I would have called you crazy. But some people actually make that their full-time job.

Whenever new inventions dramatically change the world, they create many new jobs and sometimes mean the end of others. When the Industrial Revolution occurred, which was around the late 1700s to early 1800s, the world transitioned from agriculture and human production methods to machines (National Geographic, 2023). Power Looms made clothing and large machines manufactured goods that were previously made by hand or not used at all. Factories were built to house the machinery and people looking for work slowly gravitated toward cities to find jobs at those factories. All those newly created jobs had to be done by people who were learning new skills by working there.

There were actually several "industrial revolutions." They began by driving all those machines with coal and steam, then evolved around the discovery of electricity, gas, and oil. The invention of the combustion engine (the car engine) happened alongside these (National Geographic, 2023). That's when things really got interesting because people were able to move around greater distances. Before this, it was only horses and on foot.

The third industrial revolution is also known as the *digital revolution* (Techopedia, 2019). This was the advancement of technology from analog, electronic, and mechanical devices to the digital technology we know today. It can sometimes be called the *information era*.

So why are we talking about all this history stuff? Because every time there are new inventions, it creates lots of new jobs that people learn and figure out. So, like I said, I never would have imagined people would get paid to play video games, and yet it happened. It's also pretty cool to invent them as well. That's where learning how to "code" comes in. There are lots of websites that can teach you how to code. Think of the countless number of applications available for your devices, with new ones coming out every day. Learning how to code means the ability to develop your own applications.

Influencers

So, what the heck is a social influencer? Well, these are people who somehow have gained a reputation of authority or expertise in a particular area or topic, and they use that influence to encourage their followers (GCU, 2022). They often promote things like clothes and beauty products or maybe outdoor recreation products. My son is particularly fond of a popular male influencer who gives money away to what he considers people in need. He's made a ridiculous amount of money and even travels around the country doing live shows. The more followers these people have, the more they make by sponsors and money from their sites.

The process to become an influencer is lengthy and requires the buildup of a core following. You'll need to provide entertaining content frequently to keep your followers interested. But I'm getting into the weeds here. The reason I'm talking about this goes back to the beginning of this book. What were the two things I told you to remember?

Keep your secrets safe and **don't become a victim**, right? So, if your goal happens to be something like an influencer, you're putting yourself out there in the world on display for everyone. When anyone gains popularity, there are always people who want to tear them down and see them fall. You don't have to search very far to find scandals involving influencers. Often, much of the info isn't accurate, but it still tarnishes people's reputations. If anyone has your personal information or something you may have said but regret, they will use it against you. Even if it was from years earlier, if you said something that can be used against you, it might come back to bite you later down the road. That's why it's always important to remember that what you do online is never private, so you should behave the same way you would in front of your family and teachers at school.

Tech Jobs

There are countless jobs in the technology sector. A few that might interest you include cyber security, data scientists, application developers, and virtualization specialists. I'm not going to even begin to try to list them for you, but I do want you to think about a couple of points.

First, most jobs require technology skills. Some way more than others, but the number of jobs that require tech skills will continue to increase while those that don't will decrease.

You may have heard the term STEM. It stands for Science, Technology, Engineering, and Math. Many schools have STEM programs designed to help guide kids into jobs in the field. When I first started in the tech industry, there were very few females. In fact, I was often the only female in many of the roles I held. While it's getting better and there are many more women in tech now, it's still largely occupied by males. Many companies have goals to increase their diversity numbers and so they really want to hire more women and people considered to be the minority. Girls, this is my call to you in hopes you'll find interest in the field. The tech industry is very exciting and rewarding. It changes so quickly, and we are changing the way the world works.

The other cool thing to think about is this: There are many different paths to finding jobs in tech as well. Lots of colleges have great degree programs, but there are also lots of online training programs as well. Many companies are struggling to find enough people to fill roles, so some of them often hire people who are qualified but don't have a bachelor's degree. I'm not advocating for you to avoid going to college, but sometimes there are paths that don't necessarily require a traditional 4-year degree. Talk to your parents and teachers about ways you can learn some of these skills now that will help you later.

While your parents had to go to school in a brick-and-mortar classroom, those days are also fading into the past. Today, we have technology available that makes it possible to learn from home, and you can attend school from your laptop or other digital devices. Although it's a major development in education, it's also not for everyone, so don't feel bad if you prefer going to school in a physical classroom with your friends. Even if you don't want to do all your classes online, you have the option of taking courses such as coding or learning a language. We've looked at some fun learning websites in Chapter 4.

Online schooling has become very popular since the COVID-19 pandemic in 2020, and we had to stay away from each other for a while to prevent us from getting sick. Since then, we've all gone back to our physical schools, but for some of us, it might be another option to continue doing online school.

Types of Online Schools

Online schools are different from country to country, so you and your parents will have to do some research in your country to see which options will be best for you.

This type of schooling has evolved in the United States, and the structure and implementation of the schools are different according to educational level, school district, and the individual programs that are available.

Let's take a look at some examples of online schools in the US:

- **K-12 online schools** are sponsored by states or districts and provide a flexible and accessible learning environment for students from kindergarten to twelfth grade.

- **Blended learning** happens when elements of online learning are included in traditional education. This means you can go to your classes for some instruction and then you can do the rest of your learning online.

- **Online schooling** can also help you if you have special education needs, for example, if you have a disability that makes it difficult for you to go to a traditional school.

- Colleges now also offer **degree programs online** so you can stay home and still get a degree as long as you apply yourself and do the work.

- There are also things called **certification programs and boot camps**. They aren't necessarily traditional college degrees, but they are very specialized training in particular areas and there are lots of them in technology. Many companies hire people with these certifications because they need help operating the different tech they use internally to run their company.

There are even websites that comb different sites to provide one location that can help you find the right program for you. Since there are too many for me to review, I won't list them here, but please do some of your own research and ask parents and teachers to help point you in the right direction.

Chapter Worksheet

Do you know what you might want to do for a job when you grow up?

_____

_____

Is there already a tech job that interests you or should you do some research? If so, what is it?

_____

_____

Online learning highlights

Have you had a recent learning achievement online? What did you achieve?

_____

Have you ever spent too much time watching Influencers and Gamers? What might you want to do if you had a desire to Influence others?

_____

_____

_____

Important Things You Need to Remember From This Chapter

- Technology jobs continue to increase and advance. Many of them haven't even been invented yet but will be as AI evolves.

- Don't forget no matter what you plan to do in the future, make sure nothing you do now can come back to bite you later.

- There are many ways to get introduced to technology and learn it at your own pace.

- Even kids can take online training programs for jobs in tech; it's never too early to start learning.

Chapter 9:

Who Owns Your Online Content?

Most of us love to share our cool photos and videos online, but have you really thought about who owns them once they're out there?

You usually own the stuff you create and share online, which means you can decide what you want to do with it.

Have you noticed that when you use applications and sign up for websites, you have to agree to their terms before you get an account? Before you clicked "agree," did you read their terms and conditions? Sometimes, these rules say that the platform can also use your stuff. You still own your stuff, but you've given them permission to use it as well. Sometimes, they explain that once you post, that data lives on their servers, and it's now their property.

Some creative people use something called *Creative Commons Licenses* to say how others can use their work. For example, you could tell someone that they can use your videos and photos as long as they say they're yours.

Now, when you work on projects with others, you need to talk about who owns what and who can use what. Things can get complicated, and you don't want to end up in a fight.

It's important to read and understand the rules of any website where you share your content. That way, you can make sure that your stuff stays safe.

What Is the Dark Web?

The dark web is a hidden part of the internet.

You probably know how you can search for things on the internet and find websites. Well, the dark web is different. It's not easy to find, and you can't just use a regular web browser to get there. It's not a place children should be visiting at all, but we'll talk about it in a little more detail.

You can picture the internet as being almost like an iceberg. The regular part of the internet is what you can see above the water. It's the websites and other information we can see every day. The dark web is the part that's hidden away under the water.

This hidden part contains websites and things that aren't always legal or safe.

People go to the dark web to do things secretly, like buying and selling things they shouldn't or sharing information that's not allowed. So, it's a place where you need to be very careful and not go exploring because you might find things that are not suitable for kids.

So, it's safest to keep to the regular, safe parts of the internet and always ask a grownup if you're not sure about something online.

Sometimes, people with bad intentions try to steal your personal information to sell on the dark web. It's actually a newer form of crime. They hack websites and or companies to find lots of personal data and then they use the dark web to sell it to make money. The people buying that data are planning to exploit the data they get.

People also sell personal photos on the dark web. They sometimes crawl through social media accounts to find pictures and pull them down to the dark web. So remember, whenever you post any pictures, they will never be able to be taken off the internet despite your best efforts.

Chapter Worksheet

Think about the following questions and write your answers below them. If you don't know the answers, do research or ask a grownup to help you. If you have enough information, it can help you stay safe online.

Have you agreed to the terms and conditions for using an app or website?

_____

_____

Have you ever read those terms?

_____

_____

Do you use websites and games that are suitable for your age? If not, have you received permission from your parents?

_____

_____

Do you know how to make sure your online accounts are private?

_____

_____

Have you ever shared pictures or talked about where you are online? What happened? Did you ask your parents for permission?

_____

_____

Important Things You Need To Remember From This Chapter

- When using apps and websites, you sometimes give up the rights to your content.

- Don't post anything you wouldn't want to get in the hands of the wrong people, especially personal info.

- Messages can be shared and seen by others once you've sent them.

- Try not to share photos with locations; your safety could be in danger, and they could end up on the dark web.

- You need to understand the rules of websites regarding content ownership. Your parents can help you with this, by explaining the rules to you, if you're not sure.

Chapter 10:

Location Tracking and Geo

Tagging

Location Tracking

Do you use apps to see where your friends are? If so, you're using location tracking. Almost all devices now have built-in Global Positioning System (GPS) location tracking. This is based on satellites in space that revolve around the Earth and know exactly where you are.

Many applications you use now include location tracking, which is usually helpful in providing features such as:

- Uber: picks you up and drives you where you need to go

- The weather channel: notifies you when bad weather is heading your way

- Live traffic updates: can help you avoid accidents

Knowing where your loved ones are is incredibly helpful for safety reasons, of course. My son runs cross country, and often, they are not done running when he is supposed to be picked up. I can quickly see how far from the school they are by looking at his location. Technology brings so many useful advances to enhance our lives, but it is also, at times, what's known as a *double-edged* sword (something that can both help you and hurt you at the same time). Almost all applications now track your location and many of them really don't need to. Do you have the Starbucks app on your phone? Have you ever noticed that when you go near a Starbucks location, you start getting notifications about coffee specials? Lots of apps track you so they can *market* to you and sell you something. But what are the security implications to everyone knowing where you are?

Most devices now allow you to choose individual applications that you want to allow tracking and which ones you don't. It's important to turn that off if it's not needed. This is one of those subjects you should discuss with your parents so they can help you make informed decisions. You really should only share your location with a small number of people in your life and definitely talk to your parents about who they are.

A lot of people don't know that many of the big well-known apps that collect data, are actually being managed by third party apps that are often subsidiaries. Meaning we really don't know who has access to our data and what they are doing with it.

Most devices now allow you to choose individual applications that you want to allow tracking and which ones you don't. It's important to turn that off if it's not needed. This is one of those subjects you should discuss with your parents so they can help you make informed decisions. You really should only share your location with a small number of people in your life and definitely talk to your parents about who they are.

Apps, especially social media apps, often allow you to easily check-in and tell people where you are. It's really important to be very particular about the people you choose to share you location with. This should be kept to a small number of those in your family and maybe best friends if you've received approval from parents or guardians.

Geotagged Photos

This sounds complicated, but it refers to photos that can show you where they were taken. iPhones and Android devices have this enabled automatically. When GPS is enabled, they also include this info in the metadata. Metadata is essentially extra data or additional data that describes or explains data. Sounds confusing, but as it pertains to photos, it's most often data that shows exactly where a picture was taken on a map.

When you put these photos online, people will see a map and know where your photo was taken. It's almost like telling people where you were.

The problem with this is you don't want everyone to know where you are all the time, as they might follow you on the map, and this could lead to unsafe situations.

The data is embedded into the photo and is available when you post it online. You only see the picture you post, but people who pull your picture down from the internet will have access to that data as well. You can turn this off before you share a picture online, so be sure to do your research on the type of phone you have so you know how to remove that data before you share your photos.

This can become an issue when you're on vacation and you post. As we discussed in previous chapters, it's not a good idea to let others know when your home may be empty.

Geotagging In Social Media

This is essentially letting people know where you are while using social media. Many people like to post on social media while attending an event as an example and allow Geotagged posts. While this may seem fun, it can be quite dangerous especially if you don't have your social media locked down to only show specific friends your posts.

Everyone has the right to privacy and safety. I encourage you to have a discussion with a parent about how and when it's not safe for you to let everyone know where you are all the time.

Chapter Worksheet

Think about the following questions and write your answers below them. If you don't know the answers, do research or ask a grownup to help you. If you have enough information, it can help you stay safe online.

Do you know how to choose which apps track your location?

_____

_____

Can you think of a time when you shared your location and probably shouldn't have?

_____

_____

Conclusion

By now, you would have realized that technology is one of your coolest friends that you can always carry with you. Digital devices, especially handheld ones like tablets and cell phones, are now so small and well-developed that they are like tiny computers, allowing you access to almost anything you need at your fingertips.

It helps you stay connected with your friends and you will always know what's going on in the world. You'll know all about the latest games, movies, and music available, and you'll always be on top of the latest news.

You're part of the Digital Generation (the first generation who has grown up fully digital from birth), and the development of technology has only accelerated during your lifetime. While you don't remember a time without technology, your parents and grandparents can probably tell you a lot about how they grew up without technology in the "good old days."

They could be worried that you're spending too much time online and tell you to get outside and play in nature. While you might think this isn't fun, you should take them seriously. There are a lot of benefits to using technology, but you also need to lead a balanced life and make sure you also chase your friends around outside in the physical world, and not only online.

It can be great fun to explore the digital world and try out all kinds of exciting games. There are always new apps and gadgets since technology constantly changes. It's like an ongoing, exciting adventure because there's always something new you can learn.

However, it's also important to stay safe. You will come across people online who are not kind, want to sell you something, and possibly take advantage of you.

Remember that much of the data online is not accurate and most people have an agenda. This means they are posting things they like or believe and want you to like and believe them, too. You should always look at anything you read online with a healthy dose of skepticism and do more research to see if it's true or what the opinions of others might be.

Most of the time what you see online is in some way trying to get you to click on other pages or entice you to buy something. Don't fall victim to the seemingly cool ads that promise you will get something for free if you just forward on. Nothing is free and anytime you think something sounds too good to be true, it almost always is.

Your reputation and safety are the most important parts of being a digital kid. It starts with you understanding and making good choices about what you do and say online, as well as who you interact with. Enjoy it, learn from it, and always be curious. This is a field that will always be advancing, so thinking about future jobs in technology is something to consider as well. There are so many that haven't even been invented yet but will be when you're heading off to college or wherever your path takes you.

If you liked this book, we'd love it if you could tell others about it. Your positive words can help encourage people to learn more about the digital world.

References

Artificial intelligence: What it is and why it matters. (2010). Sas. https://www.sas.com/en_za/insights/analytics/what-is-artificial-intelligence.html

Burns, E. (2022, July). *What is artificial intelligence (AI)?* TechTarget. https://www.techtarget.com/searchenterpriseai/definition/AI-Artificial-Intelligence

Dickson, B. (2023, June 5). *What is ChatGPT? A basic explainer.* PCMAG. www.pcmag.com/how-to/what-is-chatgpt-a-basic-explainer.

Duggal, N. (2023, August 21). *Advantages and disadvantages of artificial intelligence.* Simplilearn. https://www.simplilearn.com/advantages-and-disadvantages-of-artificial-intelligence-article

Duncan, A. (2020). *Educational sites that will teach your kids something new today.* Verywell Family. https://www.verywellfamily.com/best-free-educational-websites-for-kids-3129084

Emojipedia— 😀 Home of emoji meanings 🤔 👋 👍 😋. (2019). Emojipedia.org. https://emojipedia.org

Encyclopedia GIFs. (n.d.). GIPHY. https://giphy.com/explore/encyclopedia

Grand Canyon University. (2022, May 26). *What is a social influencer?* GCU. www.gcu.edu/blog/performing-arts-digital-arts/what-social-influencer.

Kodable. (n.d.). *Programming for kids.* Kodable. https://www.kodable.com/

Lawler, M. (2021, December 30). *How to do a digital detox.* EverydayHealth. https://www.everydayhealth.com/emotional-health/how-to-do-a-digital-detox-without-unplugging-completely/

Learning Resources.(n.d.). *Botley the coding robot*. Learning Resources. https://www.learningresources.com/botley-the-coding-robot

Mayo Clinic Staff. (2022, February 26). *Teens and social media use: What's the Impact?* Mayo Clinic. www.mayoclinic.org/healthy-lifestyle/tween-and-teen-health/in-depth/teens-and-social-media-use/art-20474437.

National Geographic. (n.d) *Industrialization, labor, and life*. National Geographic, education.nationalgeographic.org/resource/industrialization-labor-and-life/#

Ortiz, S. (2023, April 18). *What is ChatGPT and why does it matter? Here's everything you need to know.* ZDNET. https://www.zdnet.com/article/what-is-chatgpt-and-why-does-it-matter-heres-everything-you-need-to-know/

Osmo. (n.d.). *Award-winning educational games system for iPad*. Osmo. Www.playosmo.com. https://www.playosmo.com/en-US/

Peele, J. (n.d.). *Obama deep fake*. Ars Electronica Center. https://ars.electronica.art/center/en/obama-deep-fake/

Ricci, R. C., De Paulo, A. S. C., De Freitas, A. K. P. B., Ribeiro, I. C., Pires, L. S. A., Facina, M. E. L., Cabral, M. B., Parduci, N. V., Spegiorin, R. C., Bogado, S. S. G., Chociay, S., Carachesti, T. N., & Larroque, M. M. (2023). Impacts of technology on children's health: a systematic review. *Revista Paulista De Pediatria, 41*. https://doi.org/10.1590/1984-0462/2023/41/2020504

Rouse, M. (2017, December 12). *What is the digital revolution?* Techopedia www.techopedia.com/definition/23371/digital-revolution.

Sample, I. (2020, January 13). *What are deepfakes – and how can you spot them?* The Guardian. https://www.theguardian.com/technology/2020/jan/13/what-are-deepfakes-and-how-can-you-spot-them

SAS Analytics. (2010). *Artificial intelligence: What it is and why it matters*. Sas. https://www.sas.com/en_za/insights/analytics/what-is-artificial-intelligence.html

Schulenburg, P. (2023, May 16). *The importance of intellectual property in the digital age*. https://pagelschulenburg.co.za/the-importance-of-intellectual-property-in-the-digital-age/

Sreenivas, S. (2021, May 12). *Digital detox: what to know*. WebMD. https://www.webmd.com/balance/what-is-digital-detox

UPMC. (2019, January 6). *Is screen time really bad for our eyes?* UPMC HealthBeat. share.upmc.com/2019/01/screen-time/#:~:text=Potential%20effects%20of%20screen%20time.

What are the health benefits when kids play sports? (2021, June 30). Mayo Clinic Orthopedics & Sports Medicine. https://sportsmedicine.mayoclinic.org/news/what-are-the-health-benefits-when-kids-play-sports/

Zahid, R. (2023, June 8). *Unlocking your child's potential with AI-powered personalized learning*. Medium. https://medium.com/@rszhd/unlocking-your-childs-potential-with-ai-powered-personalized-learning-90fd9f61b13